HANDS-ON GEOLOGY

Get Hands-On with Earth's Layers!

Alix Wood

Learn all about Earth's layers with these geology projects and experiments.

PowerKiDS press.

New York

Published in 2022 by Rosen Publishing
29 East 21st Street, New York, NY 10010

Produced for Rosen Publishing by Alix Wood Books
Designed by Alix Wood
Editor: Eloise Macgregor

Consultant: Kate Spencer, Professor of Environmental Geochemistry

Cataloging-in-Publication Data

Names: Wood, Alix.
Title: Get hands-on with Earth's layers! / Alix Wood.
Description: New York : PowerKids Press, 2022. | Series: Hands-on geology | Includes glossary and index.
Identifiers: ISBN 9781725331150 (pbk.) | ISBN 9781725331174 (library bound) |
ISBN 9781725331167 (6 pack) | ISBN 9781725331181 (ebook)
Subjects: LCSH: Earth (Planet)--Core--Juvenile literature. | Earth (Planet)--
Crust--Juvenile literature. | Earth (Planet)--Mantle--Juvenile literature. |
Geology, Structural -- Juvenile literature.
Classification: LCC QE509.2 W66 2022 | DDC 551.1--dc23

Photo credits:
Cover bottom center, 1 bottom left and right, 4 bottom, 7, 11, 14 top three,
15 top right, 16 top, 18 top and middle, 19 top, 20 top and middle, 21 top four, 22, 23 top,
26, 28 top © AdobeStock Images; 4 top © Hendric Stattmann/public domain 12 top public
domain, 27 © USAF Sr. Airman Joshua Strag/public domain; all other illustrations @ Alix Wood

Printed in the United States of America

CPSIA Compliance Information: Batch #CSPK22. For Further Information contact Rosen Publishing, New York, New York at 1-800-237-9932.

Contents

Living on an Onion

Our planet, Earth, is made up of layers, a little like an onion. We live on the thin outer layer, known as the crust. Underneath the crust the layers are very different. The temperature gets hotter and the pressure gets higher as you get closer to the center of Earth.

The deepest canyons barely make a dent in Earth's crust. The Grand Canyon is just 1 mile (1.6 km) deep.

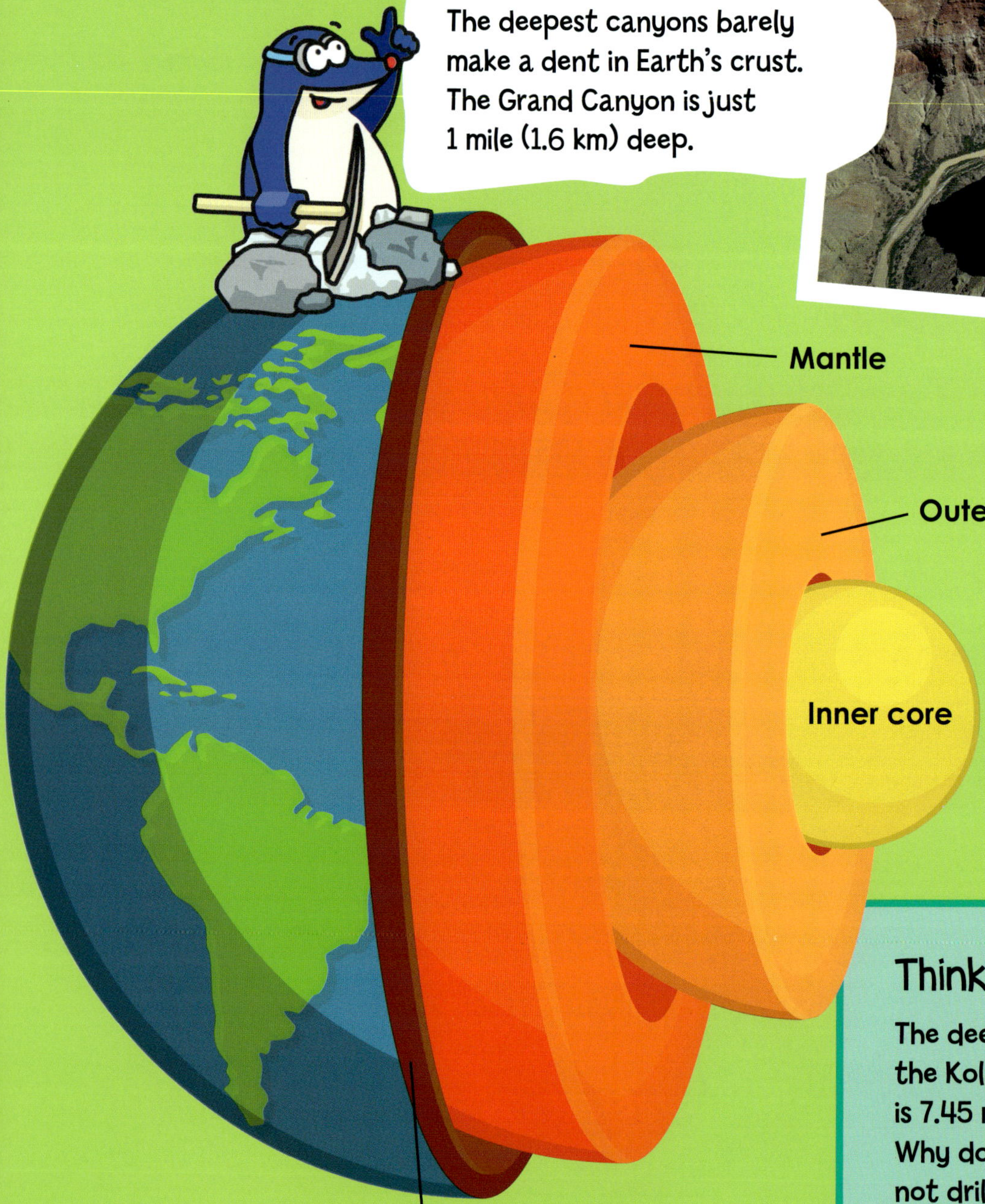

Beneath the rocky crust, the extreme temperatures in the other layers are hot enough to melt rock!

Think About This...

The deepest man-made hole, the Kola Superdeep Borehole, is 7.45 miles (12 km) deep. Why do you think people have not drilled any deeper?

How Did Earth's Layers Form?

The Earth formed around 4.6 billion years ago. Clouds of gas and dust in the **galaxy** began forming a ball. The larger the ball got, the more the force of **gravity** pulled objects toward it. Earth became a giant, hot ball of melted rock.

Slowly, Earth started to cool down. As the spinning Earth cooled, the denser materials, such as the metals nickel and iron, sank to the center and formed the core. The lighter materials, like silica and aluminum, rose to the top and formed the crust. The crust cooled and hardened. Deep underground, Earth is still full of hot melted rock.

HANDS-ON Make a Model Earth

You will need:

- some red, orange, yellow, blue, and green modeling clay (you can use colored marzipan if you like)
- a board to roll your shapes on
- a plastic knife

Keep your model Earth. You will use it later in the book.

For your core, take a small lump of red clay and roll it into a ball.

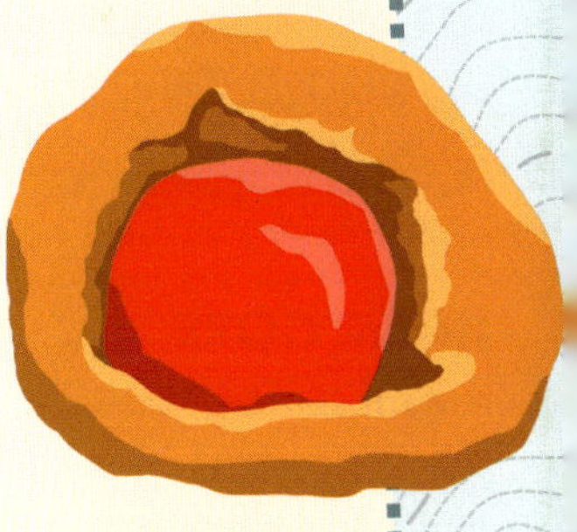

To make the outer core, press a larger lump of orange clay into a rough circle. Wrap it around the core and mold it until it covers the core entirely. Repeat the same process using a circle of yellow clay for your mantle.

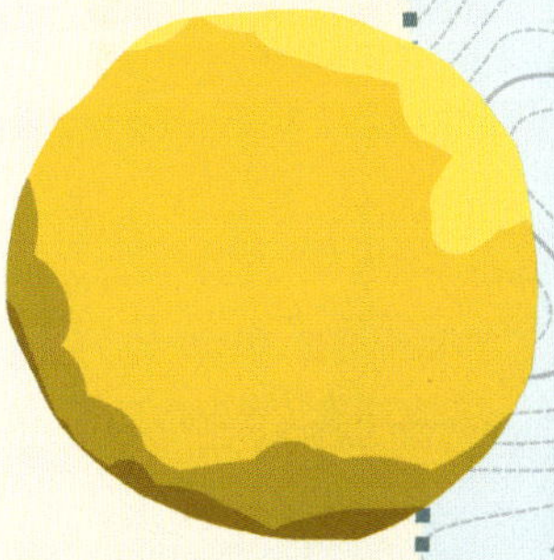

Now create Earth's crust. Make an even larger thin circle of blue clay to wrap around your model. Then take some little bits of green clay and create some areas of land. You could look at a globe if you want to make it really accurate.

Using the plastic knife, cut your Earth model in half to reveal the layers. You can push the halves together and separate them when you like.

How Thick Is Each Layer?

Compared to the total size of our planet, the tallest mountains and deepest canyons on Earth's crust are just tiny bumps and scratches! The average distance from the center of Earth's core to the surface is around 3,967 miles (6,385 km). Although the core and mantle are almost the same thickness as each other, the core makes up only 15 percent of Earth's volume. The mantle makes up 84 percent, and the crust makes up 1 percent.

Think About This...

If they are around the same thickness, why do you think the core makes up much less volume of Earth than the mantle?

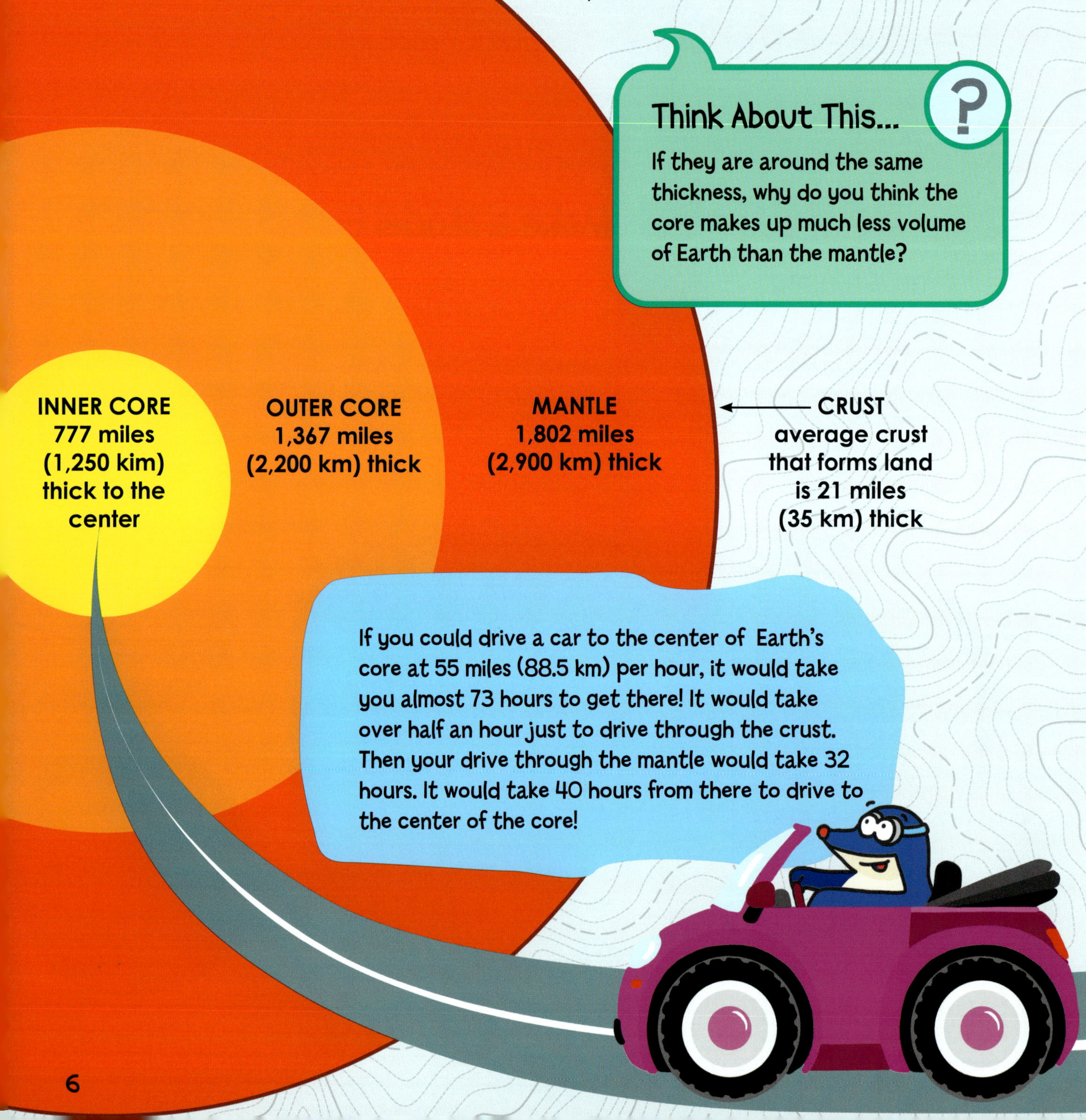

If you could drive a car to the center of Earth's core at 55 miles (88.5 km) per hour, it would take you almost 73 hours to get there! It would take over half an hour just to drive through the crust. Then your drive through the mantle would take 32 hours. It would take 40 hours from there to drive to the center of the core!

BE A GEOLOGIST
Make a Scale Model of Earth's Layers

You Will Need:

- a pair of compasses
- a pencil
- a centimeter ruler
- some colored card stock
- scissors
- a pin
- a paper fastener

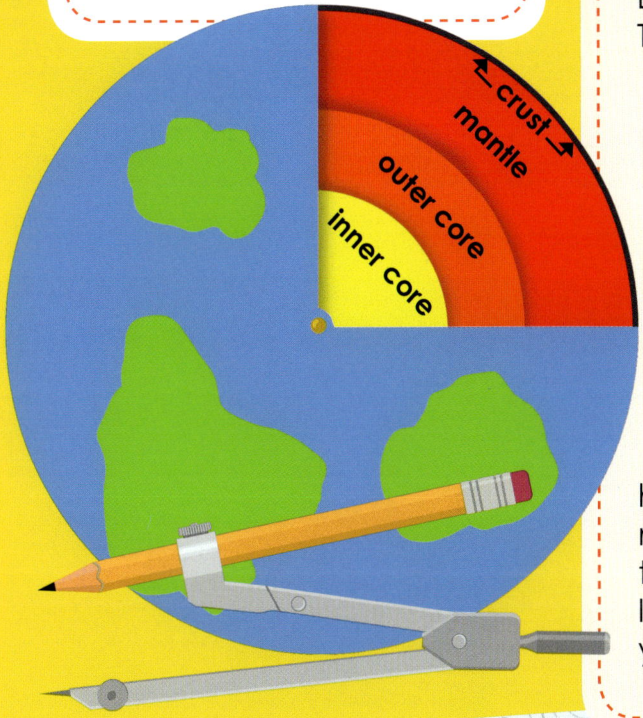

How to Make the Model:

If you have never used a compass, ask an adult to help you. For the inner core, adjust your compass opening to measure 1.25 cm, using the ruler. Poke the point of the compass into the middle of some yellow card stock. Holding the pointed end still, carefully rotate the pencil to draw your circle. Then cut it out. Do this with a different color for each layer. The compass measurements you need are:

Outer core 3.45 cm
Mantle 6.35 cm
Crust and Earth 6.38 cm

To cut the pizza slice from the Earth layer, draw a small circle around the compass hole. Draw two straight lines at right angles from that circle to the edge. Cut away the slice, carefully cutting around the little circle.

Poke a paper fastener through the compass holes in this order: Earth, inner core, outer core, mantle, crust. Decorate your Earth and label the layers. Write things you know about each layer on the hidden areas. Then you can turn your layers and reveal your facts!

HANDS-ON Chalk a Massive Earth!

You will need:

- a large area of sidewalk
- some sidewalk chalk
- a long piece of string
- a friend
- a centimeter tape measure

Use the same numbers as above to make a giant chalk Earth on your sidewalk. Just move the **decimal points** one place. Tie some chalk to one end of the string. For the inner core, measure out 12.5 cm of string and tie a knot. Ask a friend to stand on the knot. Pull the string taut and draw around with the chalk. Repeat with these measurements: Outer core 34.5 cm, Mantle 63.5 cm, Crust 63.8 cm.

Explore Earth's Layers

It's a strange fact that astronauts can travel to the moon, but we cannot explore deep inside our own planet. Why? If we traveled toward the center of Earth we would quickly die of the extreme heat. The temperature at Earth's center is as hot as the surface of the sun.

The pressure also increases because of the force of gravity. At Earth's core, the pressure is three and a half million times greater than at Earth's surface! Any vehicle we made would not survive those extreme conditions.

How Do We Know What It Is Like?

Even though we have never explored deep inside Earth, we do know quite a bit about it. How? Geologists record and study **seismic waves**. Seismic waves are caused by things like **earthquakes**, explosions, and the movement of the oceans.

There are two types of seismic waves. Shear waves (**S-waves**) can travel through solids but not liquids. Pressure waves (**P-waves**) can move through both liquids and solids. Geologists use an instrument known as a seismograph to record how waves move through Earth. The results show there must be different layers containing different material.

Think About This...

If an S-wave is recorded on the opposite side of Earth from an earthquake, what does that tell you about the layers it has traveled through?

BE A GEOLOGIST
Exploring Earth's Seismic Waves

You Will Need:

- three or four friends
- an open space

The Geology:

Seismic waves carry energy away from the center of an earthquake to the surface. The speed of the waves depends on the type of wave and the type of materials they meet. Geologists can work out if the layers the waves travel through are solid or liquid.

How to Do the Experiment:

You and your friends stand in a line, one behind the other. Each of you represents an **atom**. With your hands out in front of you, and your arms straight, grip the shoulders of the person in front. Your grip represents the **bonds** that hold atoms together in a solid.

P-wave

To mimic a pressure wave through a solid, ask the person at the back to firmly push the shoulders of the person in front. Everyone in the line should move forward, as energy is transferred from atom to atom through the bonds.

To mimic a pressure wave through a liquid, ungrip each other. Keep your arms raised, just behind the shoulders. When the person at the back pushes, the wave should still be transferred down the line.

S-wave

To mimic a shear wave through a solid, face forward and interlock arms. Ask a person at one end to step quickly forward and then back. This should produce a wobble that goes all the way down the line.

To mimic a shear wave through liquid, unlink your arms. Now, when the end person moves back and forth it does not affect the others. Having no bonds means the energy can't travel through a shear wave.

The Earth's Crust

The crust is the outer later of Earth. As Earth was forming and starting to cool, **vapor** rose from the surface. The vapor fell back down to Earth as rain. Eventually that rain formed oceans. Some of the Earth's crust became land, and some was covered by sea.

Geologists think one large mass of land, known as Pangaea, split into the **continents** that we know today. We know Earth's continents changed because fossils of sea creatures have been found in places surrounded by land. Fossils of the same animals have also been found in separate continents, hinting that they were once joined.

Think About This...

Look at the map of present-day continents. Can you see how some of them might fit together like a jigsaw?

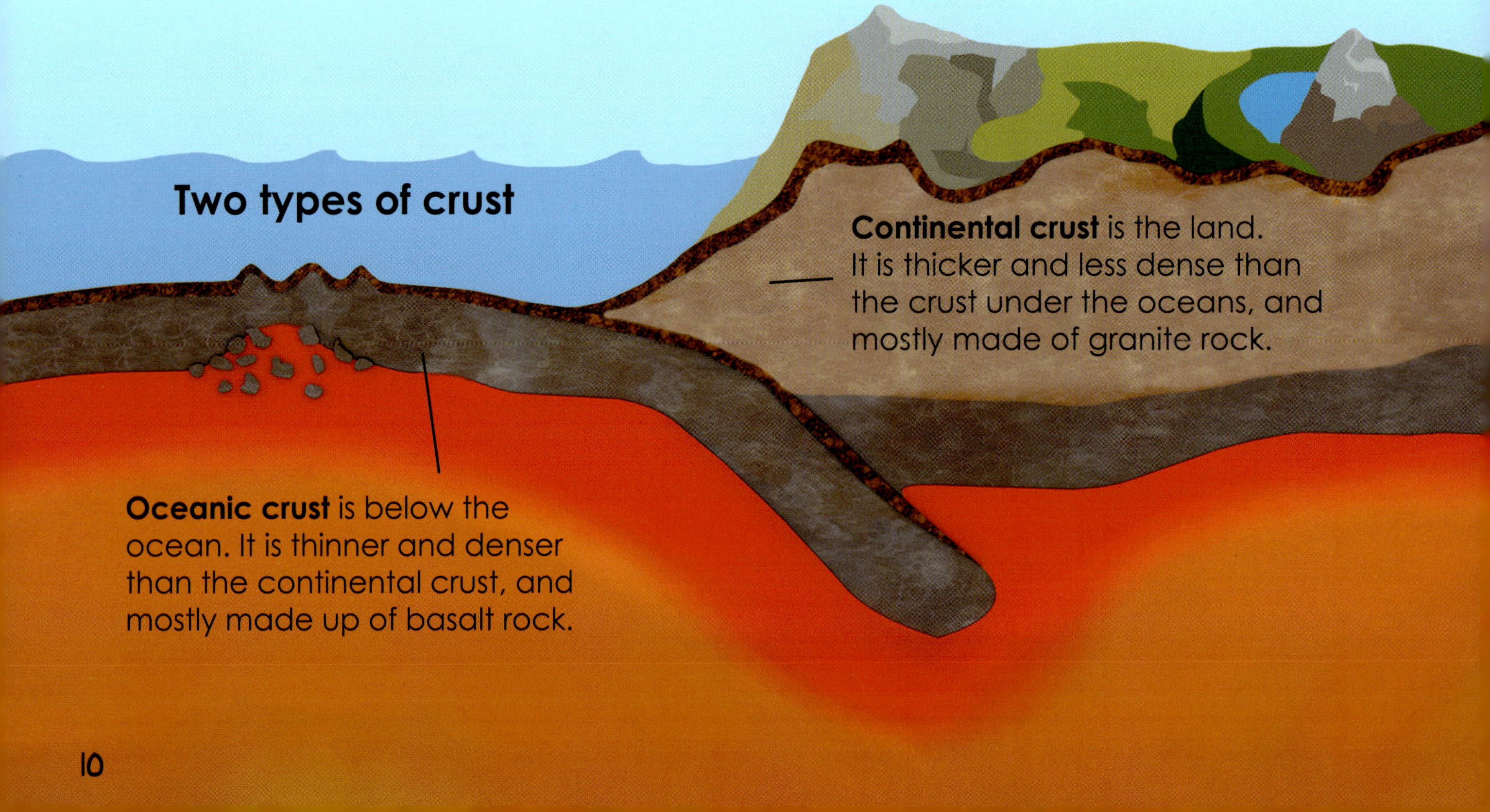

HANDS-ON How the Oceans Formed

You will need:
- a small ziplock bag
- masking tape
- some damp soil

Quarter-fill a ziplock bag with damp soil. Tape the bag onto a sunny window.

Observe what happens over a few days. As the sun heats the soil, the water will **evaporate** into a vapor. As the vapor cools, it forms clouds. When the clouds are full, the water falls as rain. This same process happened as Earth formed. Steam rose from the hot Earth, cooled, and fell as rain, forming the oceans.

BE A GEOLOGIST
Explore How Continents Move

You Will Need:

- a chocolate bar with chewy layers
- a plastic knife
- a pencil and notepad
- a camera, if you have one

The Geology:

The layers of your candy bar represent the layers of Earth. The cracks you made represent fault lines in Earth's crust. A fault line is a long crack in the surface of Earth. Earthquakes usually occur along fault lines.

How to Do the Experiment:

Using a plastic knife, make small cracks in the chocolate bar's outer layer. Draw or photograph each stage of this experiment.

Pull the ends of the bar apart. Gaps should open up at the cracks.

Push the ends of the bar together. This represents what a pressure wave might do to cracks in Earth's crust.

Now twist the ends in opposite directions. This represents what a shear wave would do.

When events such as earthquakes occur, the shifts in Earth's core affect Earth's crust.

Oceanic Crust

The oceanic crust is thinner, younger, and denser than crust under land. It is similar, though. It is made up of layers, and has mountains, valleys, plains, and volcanoes. Geologists study oceanic crust by examining rock samples, drilling into the ocean floor, and exploring the ocean bed in underwater vehicles. They also study **ophiolite**. Ophiolite is oceanic crust that has been forced up above sea level. It is easier to study than crust at the bottom of the ocean!

Ophiolite found in the Himalayas and the Alps (above) show rock from these mountain ranges were once part of an ocean floor.

Earth's crust is divided into plates. When two plates of oceanic crust move apart, molten **lava** flows up through the gap, creating new crust. Older oceanic crust is pushed outward and sinks down trenches into the mantle. This is known as **subduction**. The sunken rock is then recycled into lava. Most oceanic lava creates basalt rock. Basalt is made from tiny grains, which makes it very dense.

HANDS-ON Understanding Plates

You will need:

- peanut butter
- a wooden spoon
- two rectangular crackers
- a plate

Mimic when two plates under the ocean move away from each other. Spoon a thick layer of peanut butter onto the plate. Rest two crackers on the surface. The crackers are the plates of your oceanic crust. The peanut butter is the mantle. Press down a little on each cracker and gently pull them apart. Observe what happens. You should see some of the mantle ooze up through the gap, creating new crust or maybe even a peanut butter island! Slide one cracker under the other. This mimics the older crust being forced down into a trench.

Think About This...

What is the world's tallest mountain? It may surprise you to know it is Mauna Kea, Hawaii. Mauna Kea is only 13,803 feet (4,207 m) above sea level. Mount Everest is 29,035 feet (8,850 m) above sea level. How do you think Mauna Kea can be taller than Mount Everest?

The Atlantic Ocean is actually getting bigger. The crust beneath the Atlantic is creating new rock faster than it is losing older rock. It is growing about one inch (2.5 cm) per year. The Pacific Ocean is getting smaller. The older crust is sinking into a very deep trench, the Mariana Trench, faster than lava can create new rock.

The Moho

The boundary between the mantle and crust is known as the **Moho** after Andrija Mohorovicic, a Croatian scientist who discovered it. He realized the speed of seismic waves changed with the density of the material they moved through. This knowledge led scientists to be able to measure the depth of the crust, the point where less dense rock met the more dense mantle.

Continental Crust

About 40 percent of Earth's surface is continental crust. Continental crust is older than oceanic crust. It is lighter, so it doesn't sink into the mantle and renew itself like oceanic crust does. Some crust has been on the surface for almost as long as our planet has existed. Even rock on the continental crust renews itself, though, through the rock cycle.

Three types of rock make up Earth's crust:

Igneous rock forms when hot molten rock called **magma** cools. Granite and basalt are igneous rock.

Metamorphic rock forms from rock changed by heat and pressure deep under the surface of Earth. Slate and marble are metamorphic rock.

Sedimentary rock forms as mountains **erode** and pieces of worn rock get carried into rivers and oceans. The pieces get compressed and form rock. Sandstone and shale are sedimentary rocks.

The Rock Cycle

Forces inside Earth slowly move underground igneous and metamorphic rock to the surface, where it **weathers** and erodes. Rock fragments sink down and get heated and pressed into sedimentary rock or melted to form magma, which is forced to the surface —to start the cycle over again!

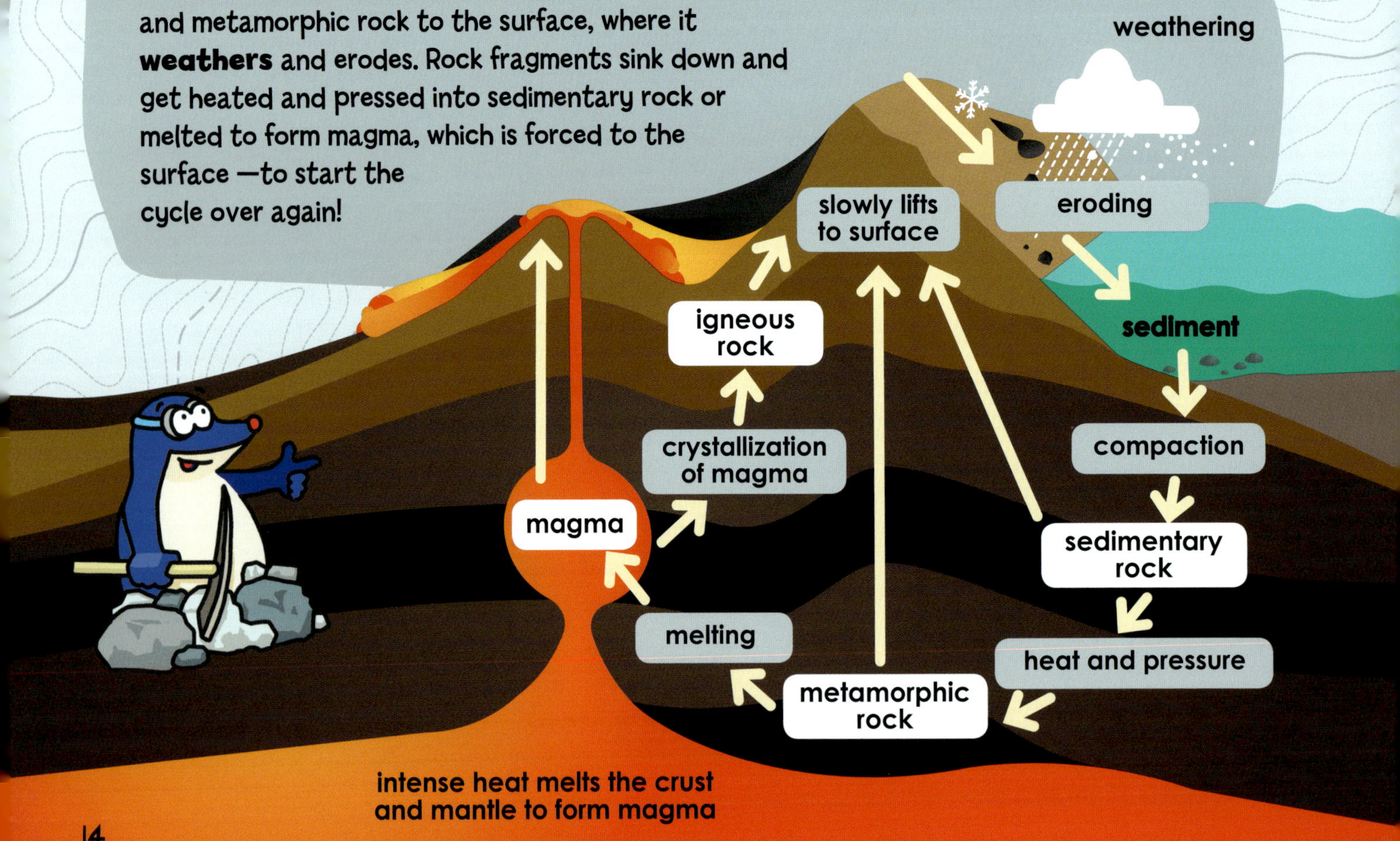

Layers upon Layers

Geologists have a law that says any rock layer underneath another layer must be older than the one above it.

Geologists sometimes draw a diagram of an area's rock layers. This helps them remember where each rock type was in relation to other layers, and helps age each layer of rock.

Think About This...

Why do you think the layers at the top are the youngest?

BE A GEOLOGIST
Make and Take a Rock Sample

You Will Need:

- several different types of bread
- some sandwich spreads
- a plastic beaker
- a spoon
- a notepad and pencil
- a camera if you have one

The Geology:

A **core sample** is taken using a drill-like tool. The tool removes a circular sample of a rock **formation** for geologists to study. A formation is a group of rock layers.

How to Make It:

Recreate a rock formation using layers of bread. You could recreate the photograph above. Perhaps use white bread for sandstone, and brown bread for basalt? For thin layers, use some sandwich spread. Try to get the thickness, texture, and color as accurate as you can in your model.

To take a core sample, place an upturned beaker on your model. Press down hard. Lift the beaker. If your core sample gets stuck in the beaker, gently pry it out using a spoon. Draw or photograph your core sample. Make a key showing what each layer represents.

Key
brown bread = basalt
white bread = sandstone
peanut butter = sediment

Finding Treasure Underground

Treasure comes in many forms. Geologists help find rock containing precious gems or metals such as diamonds or gold. They also help find precious **resources** such as water for us to drink; or coal, oil, or gas to power things. All of these resources can be found underground in Earth's crust.

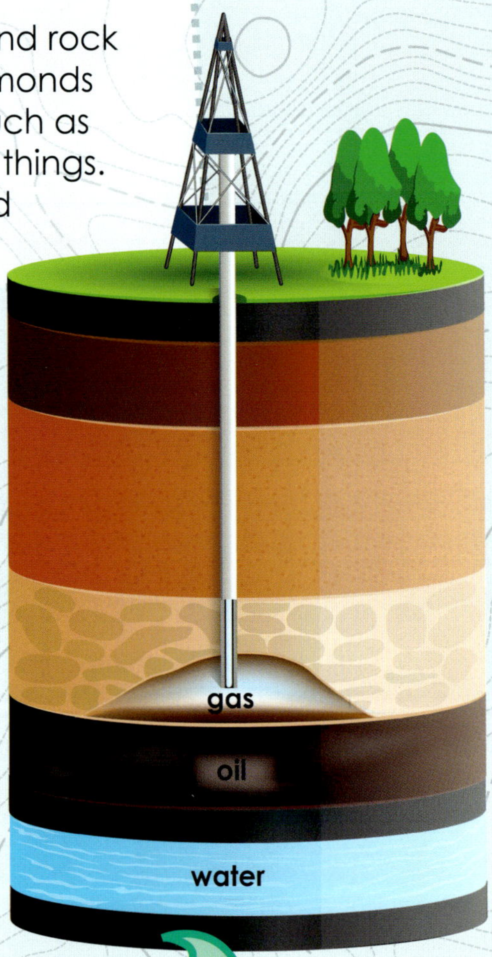

Water seeps through surface rock and is stored between layers of rock in areas known as **aquifers**. Fossil fuels, such as coal, form when **microorganisms** die, fall to the ocean floor, and become buried. Over millions of years gas, oil, or coal forms, depending on the temperature and pressure. How do geologists know where to find these hidden underground resources? They drill holes and study core samples. If the resource is found in a core sample, then it may be worth digging a mine or well there.

Think About This...

Aquifers trap water between two layers of impermeable rock. What do you think "impermeable" means?

HANDS-ON

The Water Table

You will need:

- a bucket and spade
- sand and water
- a ruler, notepad, and pencil

Quarter-fill a bucket with water. Gradually add sand until a layer covers the water. To find your water table, dig a hole until you reach a puddle. Record the height of the water level. Fill your hole back in and leave the bucket in a sunny, dry spot. Record the level again after a couple of days. Has it changed?

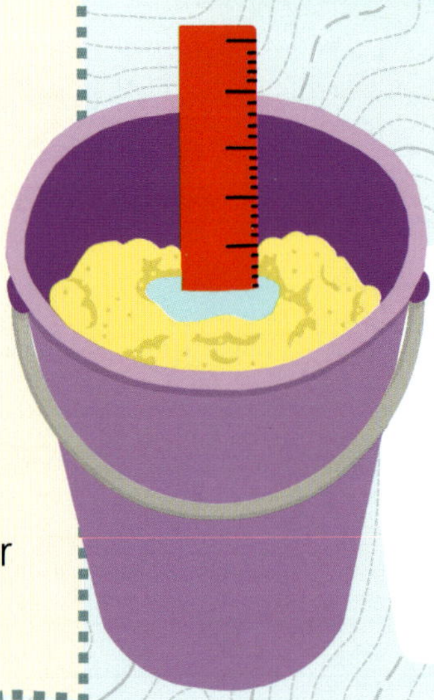

The water table is the level below which the soil is completely full of water. It can rise and fall, depending on rainfall and evaporation by the sun.

BE A GEOLOGIST
The Geological Survey Game

You Will Need:

- a friend
- different-colored modeling clay
- a straw or dry tube-shaped pasta
- a notepad and colored pencils
- some toothpicks
- masking tape

The Geology:

Rock core samples tell us a lot about what rock layers are made from, and what we may find in them. Geologist will usually take samples from more than one spot.

How to Do the Experiment:

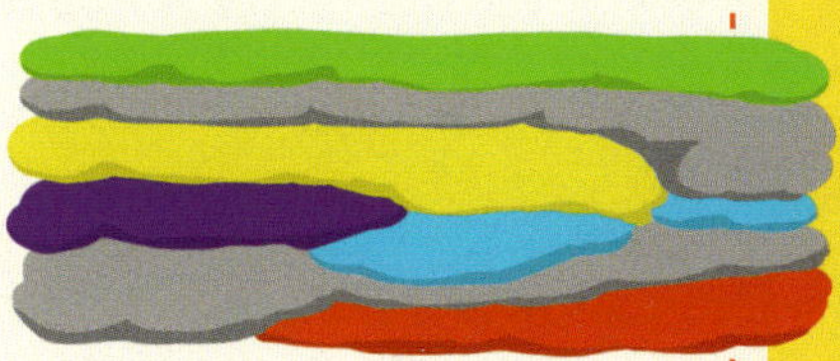

Create a model of Earth's crust, with hidden resources in the layers. Then challenge a friend to take core samples. Can they find the best place to drill for each resource?

Send your friend away while you set up the experiment. Take lumps of different-colored modeling clay and create your Earth layers. Decide what color each resource or rock layer will be. Draw a key in your notepad showing the color and what it represents. To make the game work, you need each resource to only occur in certain areas, or be different thicknesses.

Make marker flags by wrapping masking tape around the top of some toothpicks. Number each flag.

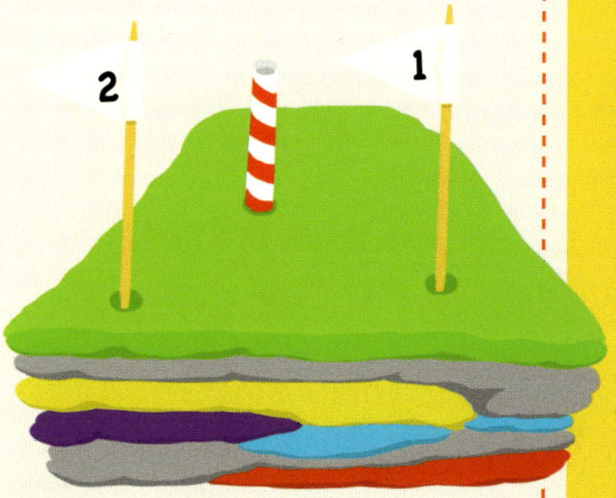

Ask your friend to come in and do their survey. To take a sample, they should push the straw or dried pasta into the clay, and then lift it out. Gently squeeze or poke each core sample out of the tube and lay it on your notepad. Give each sample a number and write it next to it. Mark where each sample was taken using the correct numbered flag.

When they have completed their survey, ask if they can tell you the best spot to drill for each resource. Then gently lift up the clay layers to check if they were right!

The Mantle

As Earth formed, the dense iron and nickel metals sank to the center to form the core. Molten material surrounding the core formed the mantle. Over time, the mantle cooled and became more solid. The mantle makes up around 85 percent of Earth's weight. It has two main layers: the upper mantle and the lower mantle.

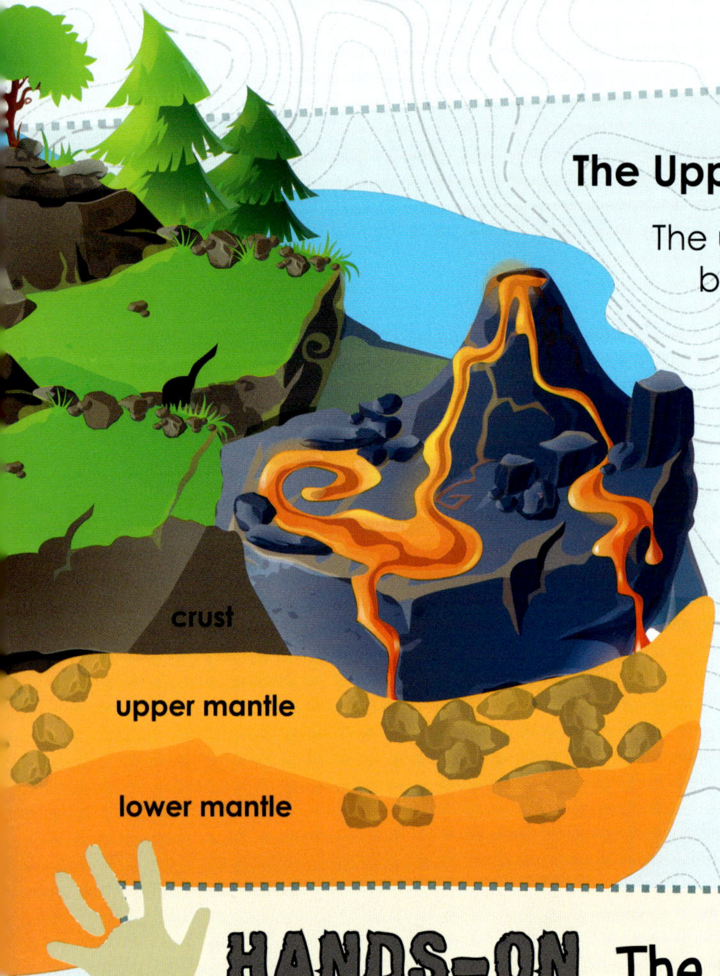

The Upper Mantle

The upper mantle is a thick layer of rock just beneath Earth's crust. Near the crust is cooler, so the rock there is firmer. The hotter lower part has both solid and melted rock.

Movement in the mantle helps shape the landscape on Earth's crust. Large slabs of rock in the upper mantle, known as **tectonic plates**, float slightly on the partly liquid mantle. Tiny plate movements cause earthquakes and volcanic eruptions, form mountains, and cause the continents to slowly move.

HANDS-ON The Upper Mantle

You will need:

- a tray
- a heavy book
- five of six marbles
- a toy animal

Put some marbles on a tray. The marbles are your upper mantle. Place a book on the marbles. The book is your crust. Put a toy animal on the book and gently tap the tray to create an earthquake. Does the crust wobble a little? Did your animal fall over?

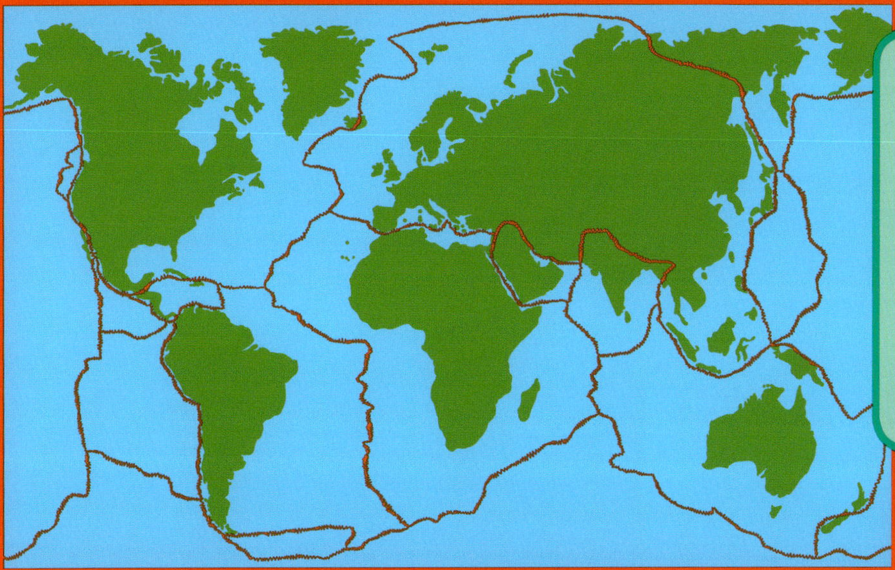

Think About This...

This map shows how Earth is divided into tectonic plates. Look at the shape of the plates and the shape of the areas of land. What do you notice?

BE A GEOLOGIST
Experiment with Tectonic Plates

You Will Need:

- a pie pan
- some water
- red or orange food color
- a polystyrene cup
- cover the floor and wear old clothes

The Geology:

It may not seem like it, but the land beneath our feet is constantly moving. It only moves from between 1 to 6 inches (2.5 to 15.2 cm) a year, though! Even these tiny movements of the mantle can cause earthquakes or volcanoes and form our mountains.

How to Make It:

Fill the pie pan with 1 inch (2.5 cm) of water. Drop a little food color into the water so it looks more like molten rock. Tear a polystyrene cup into several pieces. The pieces represent tectonic plates. Float them on the water.

Now experiment with the plates. Pull two pieces away from each other. Does molten rock fill the space between the plates? Gently bump two plates together. Could this push up the crust to form a mountain range? Or cause an earthquake?

Push one plate under another. Your colored water may squirt upward. Did it behave a little like a volcano?

Moving Layers

Earth's moving tectonic plates are on the crust and the upper mantle, together known as the **lithosphere**. The plates move very slowly, but the tiny movements cause changes to life on Earth's crust.

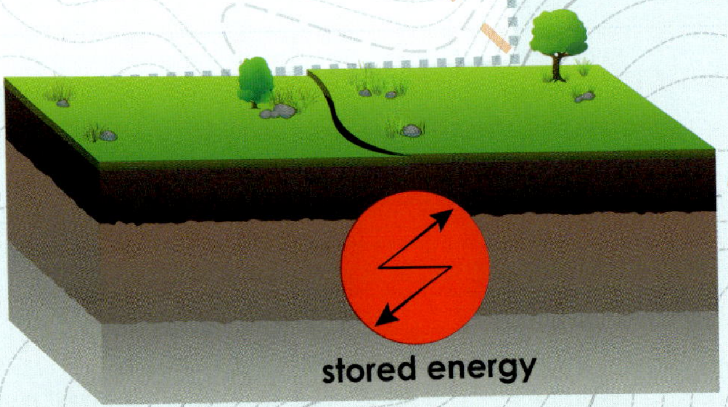

Earthquakes

Sometimes, the rough edges of two moving plates get stuck together. When the plates finally manage to slip apart, the sudden release of energy causes an earthquake. The surface where the plates slip is called a **fault**. The energy ripples outward as seismic waves that shake the ground.

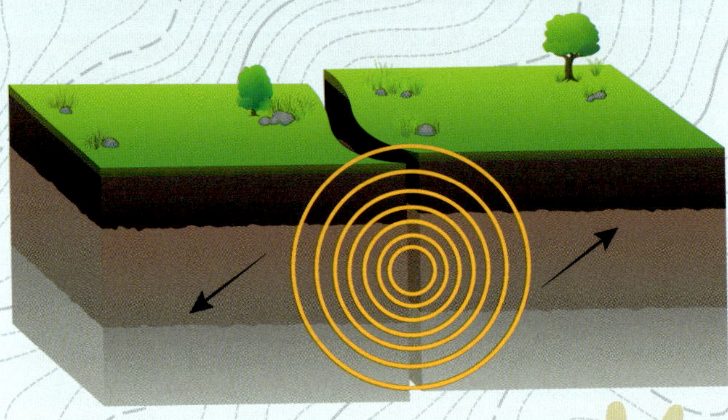

HANDS-ON Experiment with Faults

You will need:

- some cheese slices
- a few small coins

Layer four or five cheese slices on top of each other. Fold the stack in half until it splits. This split forms the edges of two tectonic plates. Place another whole cheese slice on top of the broken ones. This represents the plates sticking together.

Rest some coins on the top cheese slice. Holding a side of the stack in each hand, slowly slide your hands away from each other. Can you start to feel the tension on the top layer? That layer should suddenly give way and rip, causing your coins to wobble or fall, a little like buildings do in an earthquake.

Energy along a fault can build up and be stored for many years. Before and after a large earthquake there are often smaller earthquakes, known as foreshocks and aftershocks.

Making Mountains

Moving plates create mountains. If the plates push the crust slowly at an angle, it creates folds that form mountain ranges.

Plates can be forced up or down in blocks, forming fault-block mountains.

When magma is forced upward it creates volcanic mountains. If the magma doesn't break the surface, a dome mountain is formed.

folded mountain

fault block mountain

volcanic mountain

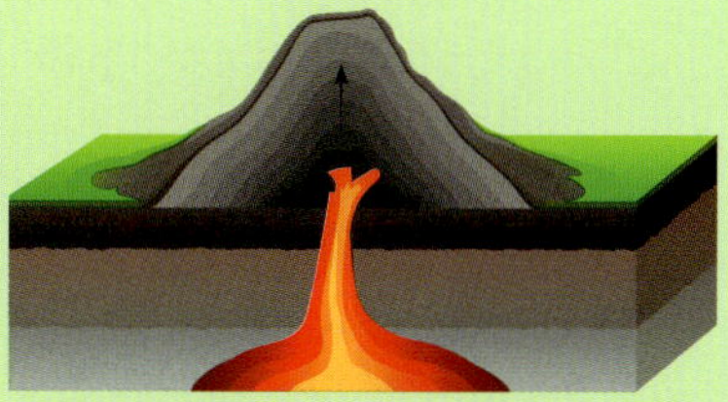
dome mountain

Think About This...

How do you think your region's mountains were formed?

BE A GEOLOGIST
Study Folded Mountain Ranges

You Will Need:

- several towels
- a friend to help you
- a camera if you have one
- a notebook and pencil

The Geology:

Your hands act like the force of moving tectonic plates. There are many different ways you can push the towels. Look at some mountain ranges. They all look slightly different for the same reason.

Make Your Mountain Range

Fold each towel in half. Lay them on top of each other to form layers. These layers represent layers of Earth's crust and upper mantle. Press a hand on each side of the towels and push them together so the towels form folds. You may want a friend to help you press one side while you press the other.

Photograph or draw your folded mountain formations. Experiment with different ways of pushing the towels together. Try only slightly pushing, or pushing at angles. Predict your result and then record what happens in your notebook.

The Lower Mantle

The lower mantle, like the upper mantle, is also made from magma. The lower mantle's magma is thicker and more solid, though. It is closer to the heat of Earth's core, so you would think its rock would be completely melted. Temperatures at the bottom of the lower mantle reach over 7,000 degrees Fahrenheit (3,871 degrees Celsius)! So why is its rock more solid?

The magma in the lower mantle is solid because of the huge pressure pushing down on it from above. Pressure in the lower mantle can reach 1.3 million times the pressure on Earth's surface!

This pressure turns rock into minerals that could not be created on Earth's crust. How do we know what rock exists deep in the lower mantle? Geologists figure that out by looking at rock thrown out of erupting volcanoes. Volcanic rock comes from deep inside the mantle. Geologists know from this that the lower mantle is rich in iron, oxygen, silicon, aluminum, and magnesium.

aluminum

HANDS-ON

Volcanic Rock

obsidian

See if you can find some volcanic rock at a local museum or rock shop, or look at some pictures on geology websites. When magma cools and hardens on the surface it forms a type of rock that is almost glassy in texture. Obsidian is a type of rock formed in this way.

granite

When magma cools and hardens underground it forms grainy rocks such as granite and gabbro.

BE A GEOLOGIST
How Pressure Affects the Mantle

You Will Need:

- a notepad and pencil
- a measuring cup
- a plastic cup
- water
- cornstarch
- a bowl
- a spoon

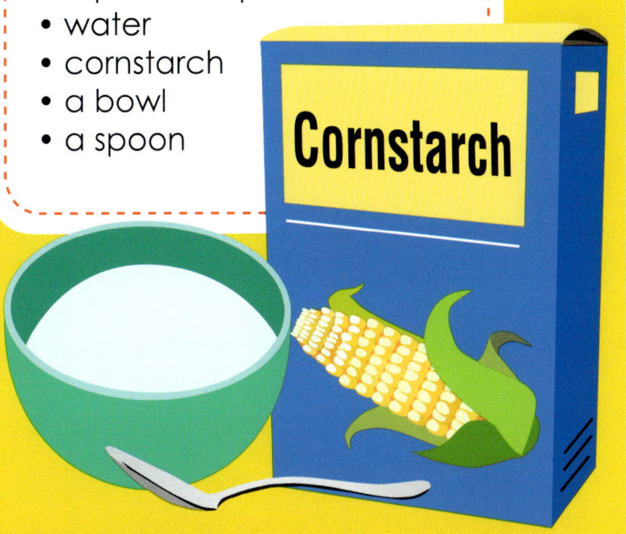

How to Do the Experiment:

Pour half a cup of water into the plastic cup. Gradually add cornstarch, one tablespoon at a time. Stir the water after each spoonful. Keep adding cornstarch until the mix becomes hard to stir.

Do you think you will be able to pour this mixture out of the cup? Try it. Tip the cup gently over the bowl and see if you can pour it. Make notes about how the mixture behaves when you pour it quickly, or slowly.

What happens to the mixture if you press it? Try to scrape the last bits out of the cup using the spoon. Does the mixture stay as a free-flowing liquid?

IMPORTANT–When you have finished your experiment, wrap the fluid in newspaper and put it in the trash. It will block your drain if you pour it down the sink.

The Geology:

In the lower mantle, the rock can be both liquid and solid. How can that be? A little like our cornstarch experiment, the rock flows easily when it is not under pressure. When the rock is under pressure, it hardens.

The cornstarch mixture is what is known as a **non-Newtonian fluid**. This fluid acts like a liquid when poured, but acts like a solid when a force is acting on it. Try grabbing some of the mixture. It will quickly harden under the pressure, and then slowly ooze out of your hands.

Think About This...

Quicksand is also a non-Newtonian fluid. It changes based on how much and at what speed a force is applied. What do you think the best way to escape quicksand would be? Try testing your theory using a plastic toy in your bowl.

The Outer Core

The outer core lies between the inner core and the mantle. It is made up of liquid iron and nickel. This layer of Earth plays an important part in protecting our planet from harmful **solar flares** and strong winds coming from the sun. How can a layer deep under Earth's crust help protect us from the sun?

The liquid iron and nickel spin as Earth rotates around its **axis**. As it does so, it turns Earth into a giant magnet and creates Earth's magnetic field. Earth's North Pole and South Pole are **poles** of this huge magnet!

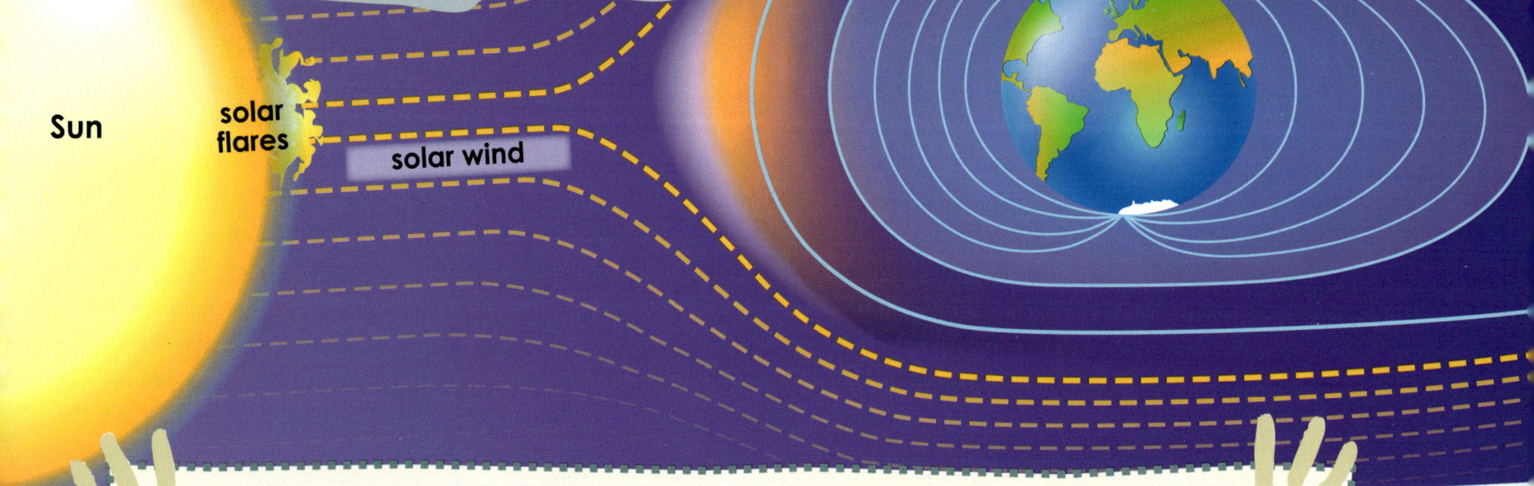

HANDS-ON Make a Magnetic Earth

You will need:

- a bar magnet
- a straw
- your clay model of Earth
- a small compass

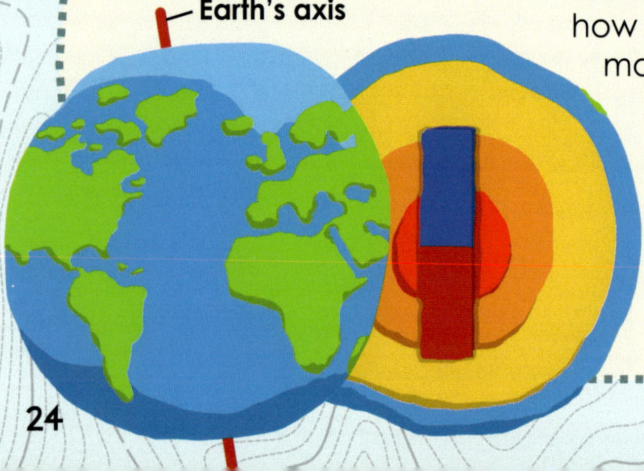

Use the modeling clay Earth you made on page 5 to make your magnetic Earth. Split your Earth in half. Press a bar magnet into one half from North to South. Press a straw in the other half. Mold your model closed again. Move your compass around Earth and watch how the needle reacts. Did you put your bar magnet the right way around?

Earth's magnetic field does not line up exactly with the axis. Magnetic poles move a little. The magnetic North Pole is close to Earth's axis now, but a hundred years ago, it was in Arctic Canada!

BE A GEOLOGIST
Looking at Magnetic Fields

You Will Need:

- a bar magnet
- iron filings (from hardware store)
- a large piece of white paper
- pencil or pen
- a small compass

The Geology:

Even though magnetic fields are invisible, you can see them by seeing the effect they have on some objects. Field lines circle out from the North Pole back to the South Pole. Earth's magnetic field acts like a shield, protecting Earth from gases and particles that would harm our atmosphere.

Think About This...

We believe migrating birds use magnetic fields to find their way!

How to Do the Experiment:

Place the bar magnet in the center of a large piece of paper. Trace around the magnet and mark north and south.

Put the magnet back in position. Place the compass at the corner of one end. Mark a pencil line next to the compass arrow, in the direction it is pointing.

Move the compass so the base of its arrow points to the line you've just made. Mark a new line where the arrow is now pointing. Connect the lines to draw the magnetic field line. Repeat the process from different spots along the magnet to make more field lines.

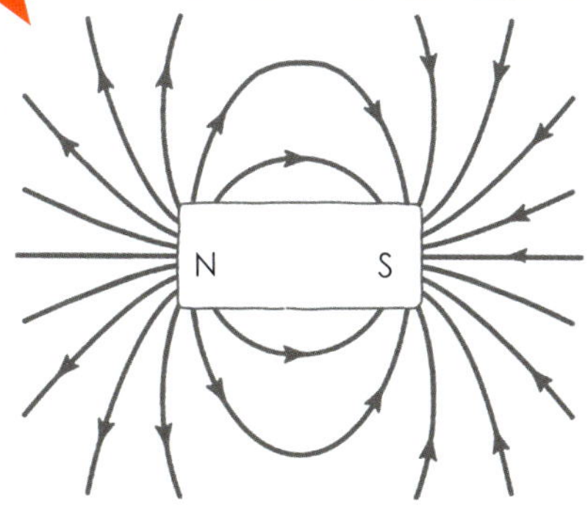

Here's another cool way to see field lines. Place your magnet back in position, but under the paper. Sprinkle iron filings on the paper. Tap the paper gently. The filings will position themselves along the field lines you drew!

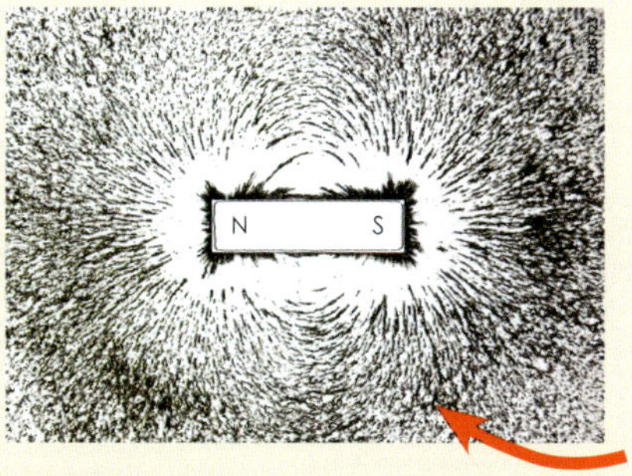

How the Outer Core Affects Life on Earth's Crust

Earth is gradually cooling and in billions of years' time the outer core will become solid. Life on Earth would be impossible for many reasons, one of which is that a cold outer core would mean we would lose our important magnetic field.

The magnetic field helps protect Earth's atmosphere from blasting by solar wind.

The magnetic field helps birds and animals find their way around.

Heat escaping from the outer core causes volcanic eruptions. Eruptions actually help make fertile soil to grow our food, and produce gases that we breathe.

Without a magnetic field, compasses will all stop working.

The magnetic field bounces dangerous radiation from the sun back into space. Without it, our planet would overheat, and the oceans would disappear.

Think About This...

Saturn, Jupiter, Neptune, and Uranus have magnetic fields even stronger than ours. What does that tell us about the inner layers of these planets?

When tiny particles from the sun hit Earth's magnetic field, the energy can cause amazing colors of light, called an **aurora**. Auroras occur most often around the North Pole (aurora borealis) and South Pole (aurora australis). Why? Earth's magnetic field guides the incoming particles toward the poles.

BE A GEOLOGIST
Make Your Own Compass

You Will Need:

- a magnet
- a needle
- piece of polystyrene
- a large bowl of water
- a pencil and notebook

The Geology:

A compass needle will point north. Oddly, that has not always been true! Through time, the poles have reversed, so that magnetic north was magnetic south! These reversals are recorded in rocks with iron-bearing minerals. The minerals are like tiny magnets floating in the molten rock, and they align to the magnetic field. As the rock becomes solid, the minerals are still locked to that magnetic field.

How to Make a Compass:

Find a piece of polystyrene foam, perhaps a tray from some food packaging. Make sure it is clean. Cut a small piece of the foam and float it in a large bowl of water.

To magnetize your needle, rub the magnet along the needle around 50 times, in the same direction. Carefully place your needle on the foam in the bowl. Observe and record what happens.

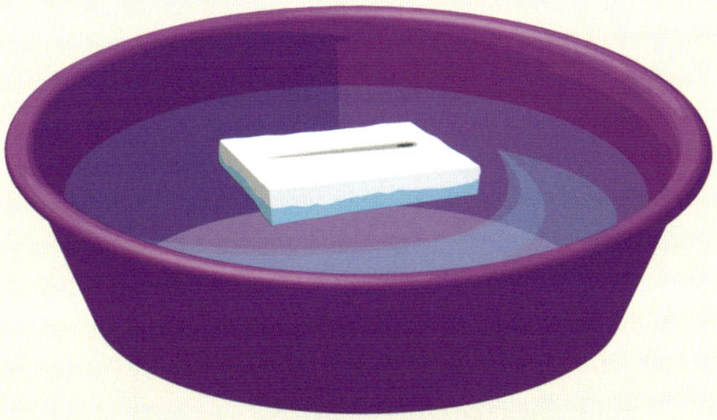

Try moving the bowl around. Does your needle always point in the same direction? Do you know which direction it pointed?

The Inner Core

The inner core is the deepest layer on Earth. This metal ball made of iron and nickel is almost as hot as the surface of the sun. Despite being so hot, the inner core is solid, because the pressure in the core is over a million times more than the pressure on Earth's surface.

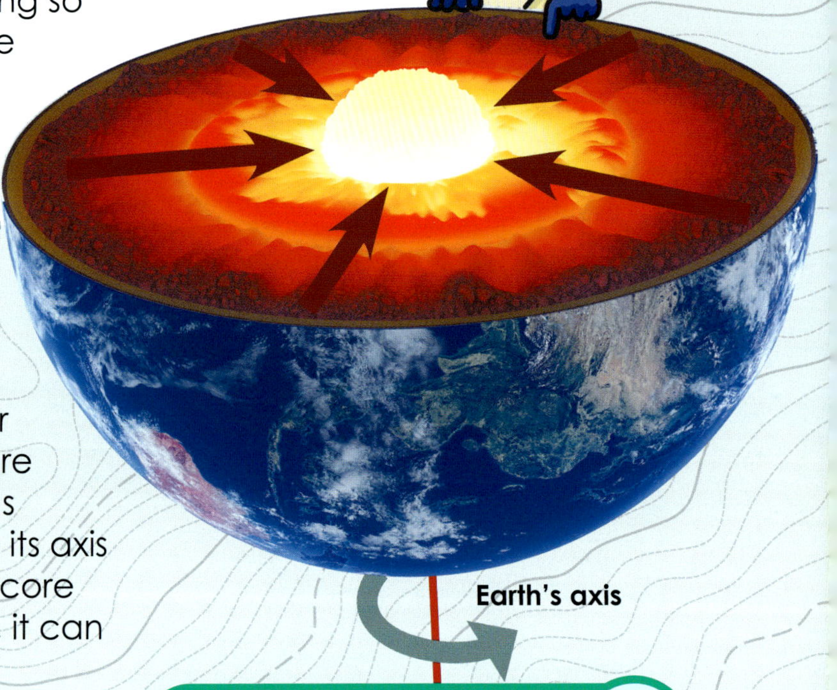

The inner core rotates faster than the rest of Earth. Scientists studying shock waves from nuclear explosions discovered the inner core moves a fraction faster than Earth's surface. Earth completes a turn on its axis about every 24 hours. As the inner core floats inside the molten outer core, it can turn at a different speed.

If you stood on a spot along the equator on the same day, two years running, the part of the inner core that was under you the first year would be 4.8 miles (7.7 km) away!

Think About This...

How long do you think it would take for the rotating inner core to overtake the crust?

HANDS-ON Model a Spinning Earth

You will need:

- a small lollipop
- a large marshmallow
- a teaspoon

The lollipop represents the solid inner core. The marshmallow represents the molten outer core.

Make a small slit in the top of the marshmallow using the end of a teaspoon. Carefully push the lollipop into the hole, so the candy is completely covered by the marshmallow.

Hold the stick between both palms. Slowly roll the lollipop stick between your hands. Observe what happens to the wobbly marshmallow. Do you think it spins at the same speed as the solid lollipop core?

Geologists know the inner core is solid from studying earthquakes' shear waves and seeing them travel from one side of Earth to the other. As we know shear waves cannot travel through a liquid, geologists are sure the inner core must be solid.

They also know the core is changing. The whole of Earth's core was molten when Earth first formed. As Earth cooled, a solid inner core was created. That solid area has been growing in size ever since, as the Earth continues to cool. The inner core grows about 0.039 inch (1 mm) a year.

BE A GEOLOGIST
Make an Edible Planet Earth!

You Will Need:

- a hard candy
- a marshmallow
- chocolate chip ice cream
- chocolate shell sauce, chopped nuts, or sprinkles
- a bowl
- a teaspoon
- a plastic knife

The Geology:

Each edible layer is quite a good representation of Earth's layers – and it tastes good!

How to Make the Layers:

To make your inner and outer core, push a hard candy inside a marshmallow, just as you did for the spinning Earth.

For the mantle, make a large ball of ice cream. Cut it in half using the plastic knife. Scoop out enough space to fit your core inside. Then press the other half of the ice cream ball quickly back in place.

To make your Earth's crust, try using chocolate shell sauce. The sauce hardens when poured onto frozen ice cream. Put your Earth in the freezer for 15 minutes, then take it out again. Pour the sauce over the Earth and let it harden. Or roll your ice cream ball in a bowl of sprinkles or chopped nuts.

Now you can eat your planet!

IMPORTANT–Be sure to warn people that there is a hard candy hidden in the marshmallow. You can choke on candy.

Glossary

aquifers an underground water-bearing layer of rock.

atom the smallest particle of an element, having all the characteristics of that element.

aurora broad bands of light that have a magnetic and electrical source and that appear in the sky at night.

axis a straight line about which a body or a geometric figure rotates.

bonds how atoms are held together.

continental crust the relatively thick part of Earth's crust that forms the large land masses.

continents the great divisions of land.

core sample a cylindrical section of rocks, soils, or sediments.

decimal points the dots in decimal numbers.

earthquakes shakings or tremblings of a portion of Earth's surface.

erode to wear away by or as if by the action of water, wind, or glacial ice.

evaporate to turn into vapor from a liquid state.

fault a break in Earth's crust.

galaxy one of the very large groups of stars and other matter that are found throughout the universe.

gravity a force of attraction between particles or bodies that occurs because of their mass.

igneous rock rock formed by hardening of melted Earth.

lava molten rock coming from a volcano.

lithosphere the outer part of Earth made up of the crust and part of the mantle.

magma molten rock material inside Earth.

metamorphic rock a rock changed from its original form by temperature and pressure.

microorganisms extremely tiny organisms such as bacteria.

Moho the Mohorovicic discontinuity is the boundary layer between Earth's crust and mantle, the depth of which varies.

non-Newtonian fluid a liquid that can change when under force to either more liquid or more solid.

oceanic crust the relatively thin part of Earth's crust that underlies the ocean basins.

ophiolite a section of Earth's oceanic crust and the underlying upper mantle that has been uplifted and exposed above sea level.

poles one of two or more regions in a magnetized body at which the magnetism seems to be concentrated.

P-waves waves that shake the ground back and forth in the same direction and the opposite direction as the direction the wave is moving.

resources a usable stock or supply.

sediment material such as stones and sand deposited by water, wind, or glaciers.

sedimentary rock rock formed by or from sediment.

seismic waves elastic waves generated by an earthquake or an explosion.

solar flares a brief eruption of intense high-energy radiation from the sun's surface.

subduction the sideways and downward movement of the edge of a plate of Earth's crust into the mantle beneath another plate.

S-waves waves that shake the ground back and forth perpendicular to the direction the wave is moving.

tectonic plates massive slabs of solid rock, generally made of both continental and oceanic lithosphere.

vapor a substance in the gaseous state.

weathers changes by the actions of the forces of nature.

Further Information

Museums and Places to Visit

Mining Museums Your area may have a mining museum or visitor center where you can find out about minerals that occur locally underground.

Science Museums will often have information about the geology of Earth, and may have exhibitions about earthquakes and volcanoes.

Useful Websites

This National Geographic Kids website has information about the features of each of Earth's layers.
https://www.natgeokids.com/uk/discover/geography/physical-geography/structure-of-the-earth/

The Science for Kids website is full of easy-to-understand facts and diagrams about Earth's layers.
https://www.scienceforkidsclub.com/earths-layers.html
This Science for Kids link has information about Earth's magnetism.
https://www.scienceforkidsclub.com/earths-magnetism.html/

Books to Read

Hutmacher, Kimberly. *Studying Our Earth, Inside and Out*. Vero Beach, FL: Rourke Educational Media, 2019.

Throp, Claire. *A Journey to the Center of the Earth*. Oxford, UK: Raintree, 2015.

Publisher's note to parents and teachers: Our editors have reviewed the websites listed here to make sure they're suitable for students. However, websites may change frequently. Please note that students should always be supervised when they access the internet.

Index